THE ST. JOHN BEACH GUIDE

The Complete Guide to the Beaches on the
Island of St. John in the United States Virgin Islands

By Gerald Singer

THE ST. JOHN BEACH GUIDE

The Complete Guide to the Beaches on the Island of St. John
in the United States Virgin Islands

By Gerald Singer

Published by: Sombrero Publishing Co.
                  PO Box 1031
                  St. John USVI   00831

© 1994 by Gerald Singer
First Printing 1994

Illustrated by Les Anderson
Cover design by Katydids
Cover photo by Don Kreuter
Maps by John Campbell

Printed in the United States of America

Library of Congress Catalog Card Number 94 - 66624

ISBN # 0-9641220-0-6

"... out to the windy beach,
Far from the twisted reach
of crazy sorrow..."

- Bob Dylan, *Hey Mr. Tambourine Man*

Table of Contents

Foreword

Authoritative sources indicate that the Foreword for a book is a "seldom read 'pitch' for the book". Do you read Forewords? I usually don't. They're boring. And who wants to read a "pitch" for a book you're already reading, anyway?

However, if you've read this far, either you are very bored with absolutely nothing better to do right now, you are on vacation in a truly relaxed frame of mind, or both. In any event, authoritative sources say you are expecting a preview, a pitch, an enticing glimpse of what's waiting for you between the covers of *The St. John Beach Guide*. Well, here you are.

When I first came to St. John and visited the beaches, I was amazed. The beaches looked just like the pictures in the travel brochures, and the fancy ads in magazines. The water was the same ridiculously rich blue, the sand as white; and the sun danced on both, creating the same clean shimmers and shadows which looked so enticing from cold, rainy New England.

Ski areas never have as much snow when you visit as they show in their brochures. The salad bar at Wendy's never quite matches it's drooling portrayal in the TV commercials. Movies are rarely as good or exciting as their previews. But to dive into the clear, sun drenched water at Hawksnest Beach on a Sunday morning, and feel the refreshing water slip, slide and smooth all around your body,... is way better than the brochures. Open your eyes under water, swim to the bottom, and dig into the soft sand. Get a mask and snorkel. The fish and coral more than match the brochures.

Any visitor to St. John wishing to enjoy "brochure" quality experiences, will benefit from the information contained here in this book. Visitors looking for alternative, unconventional or esoteric beach experiences, will also find Mr. Singer's book a valuable read.

If you are old or tired, this book will guide you to the beaches with easy access and facilities.

If you are active, this book will challenge you with Action Notes.

If you are inquisitive, this book will tell you all sorts of interesting things, like how Rendezvous Bay got its name, and what a turpentine tree looks like.

If you are confused and lost, this book will give you clear directions.

If you are in need, this book will show you how to make your wishes come true. (see page 59)

So, in the true spirit of a Foreword, I heartily encourage you to buy, read, and enjoy this book. And do stop reading Forewords.

John Campbell, February 14, 1994

Acknowledgement

Thanks to:

John and Jen Campbell for the action notes.

Dan Silber, Isaak Aronson and John Campbell for proofreading .

Bob Medori for promotional information.

Carol Stoddard for typesetting information.

Fran Attard for ideas and information.

John Gibney for historical information and material on the north shore beaches.

Tal Carter for help on the Hawksnest Bay section and who was with me when I first began this guide.

Mary Blazine, David Crowell and Kate for help on the East End chapter.

Bob Gross and Ross Singer for assistance on the Coral Bay section.

Christine Singer who contributed to the Hansen Bay section.

Jimmy Oyola for information on Frank Bay.

Roger Harland who contributed his words of wisdom.

Jennifer Stahl (The world's greatest authority on the more esoteric aspects of St. John's beaches) who worked with me on the East End, Peter Bay and Little Cinnamon sections.

Old friends with whom I first explored these beaches many years ago:

John Gibney

Calis Sewer

Charlie Deyalsingh (Trinidad Charlie)

Andy and Janet Rutnik

Les Anderson

Dan Kowalski (Ski)

Herman Smith

Dan Silber

Rupert Marsh

Bob and Nina Gross

Victor Hall

Rafe Boulon

Tal Carter

Eddie Johnson

Joe Rubino (Hippie Joe, Moses, Jesus)

Art Albricht (Crazy Art, Art D'Painter)

Basil Harley

Introduction

St. John is truly a beach lovers dream come true. Here are some helpful hints to ensure your enjoyment of our wonderful beaches, and to ensure that others for generations to come will have the same opportunity .

Be polite and respectful to the local people. It is customary in the Virgin Islands to greet people on both formal and informal occasions. When you meet someone on the beach or in town, or if you are about to have business dealings with someone, always begin your conversation with "Good morning, Good afternoon or Good night" (in the Virgin Islands "Good night" is a greeting). The local people here are very friendly and helpful. Getting to know some of them can be extremely rewarding and will greatly add to your enjoyment of St. John. Don't be afraid to initiate a conversation.

Be careful of the tropical sun. Remember to use sun block and think about covering up after a while especially if you are newly arrived to the islands. It also may be a good idea to bring something to drink if you are going to a beach without a snack bar, restaurant or store.

Always wear a shirt in town or on the ferry. Bare chests for men and bikini tops for women are not allowed in public places.

Try to avoid sea urchins, jelly fish and fire coral.

Please don't litter.

When diving or snorkeling, don't touch the coral. Even though the coral reefs seem hard, they are very fragile and can be damaged easily. The coral will regenerate, but the process is slow. Some varieties grow just a few centimeters per year.

It is against the law to spearfish or to be in possession of spearfishing equipment in the National Park waters. Spearfishing of lobsters is prohibited throughout the Virgin Islands.

If you are coming to the beaches by boat, try to tie up to a National Park mooring if they are available. If not, anchor in sand well away from coral reef.

Dogs are not allowed on National Park beaches, campgrounds or picnic areas, or on any other beaches that are marked with swim buoys.

CHAPTER ONE

The North Shore Beaches

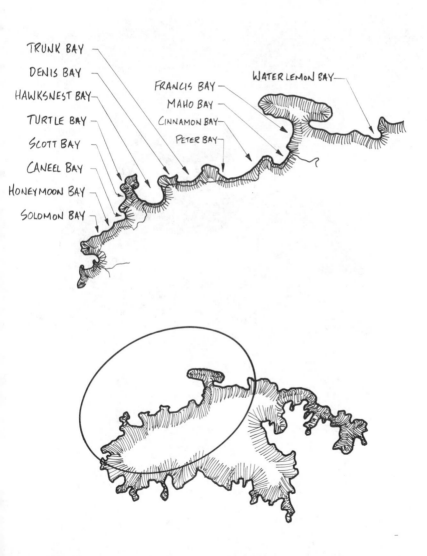

TRUNK BAY
DENIS BAY
HAWKSNEST BAY
TURTLE BAY
SCOTT BAY
CANEEL BAY
HONEYMOON BAY
SOLOMON BAY

FRANCIS BAY
MAHO BAY
CINNAMON BAY
PETER BAY

WATER LEMON BAY

SOLOMON BAY

How To Get There:

Leaving Cruz Bay, go north past Mongoose Junction and up the hill on the North Shore Road (Route 20). Turn left at the top of the hill, just before the Virgin Island National Park sign. Drive to the end of the road and park. The trail to the beach is on the right side of the dead end between a trailer house and a park service building. Go down the trail about 50 yards and turn right at the intersection of the main Lind Point Trail. (This trail originates near the Visitors Center in Cruz Bay, and the hike may be started from there as well.) Go 50 yards more, then turn left and continue down the trail which ends at Solomon Beach. (about 400 yards)

Description:

Solomon Bay is the first (closest to Cruz Bay) of the famous north shore beaches which are characterized by soft white sand and coconut palm fringed shorelines. The bottom is soft sand, the water is crystal clear and the view is spectacular.

Facilities: None

Comments:

The trail to Solomon Bay is well maintained by the National Park, and the foliage is beautiful. You will see turpentine trees, with their characteristic reddish bark and turpentine smell. You will also observe stands of West Indian birch, used in making fish traps, false pineapples and various varieties of palms. Up in the trees you may see large brown nests, some nearly four feet in diameter, with long brown trails that wind down the trunk. These are termite nests. Many of the trees also contain air plants, orchids and anthuriums. These same air plants will also be found among the many beautiful rock formations that are visible along the trail.

Mountain doves are plentiful in the area, especially in the early morning.

Pillsbury Sound is visible almost in it's entirety from this beach. Starting from the west, you can see the islands of St. Thomas, Thatch Cay, Grass Cay, Mingo Cay, Lovango Cay, Durloe Cay, Henley Cay and Jost Van Dyke.

There is good snorkeling between Solomon Bay and Honeymoon Bay to the east. The proximity of the reef and the soft sandy bottom, characteristic of Solomon and other north shore beaches, make them ideal for beginning snorkelers.

Solomon Bay is spelled "Salomon Bay" on the nautical charts. The National Park sign, however, is spelled "Solomon Bay" and this is also the current pronunciation.

Because of the relative difficulty in getting to this beach it is often much less crowded than the other north shore beaches.

Action Note:

The world record running from Solomon beach to the parking lot is 1 minute 42 seconds. Women's record is 2 minutes 12 seconds. Go for it!

HONEYMOON BAY

How To Get There:

Follow the directions to Solomon Bay, but continue east on the Lind Point Trail instead of turning left at the Solomon Bay spur. Another option is to go to Solomon Beach, walk to the other end (east), and continue on around a small point. Honeymoon will be the next beach.

For those who want an easier route, Honeymoon Bay can also be reached by approaching from Caneel Bay Resort. (See directions to Caneel Bay.) You must first go to the Day Visitor Registration Booth and inform them that you would like to go to Honeymoon Bay. They'll give you directions for the easier, though slightly longer, walk to the beach.

Description:

Honeymoon Bay is a coconut palm fringed, white soft sand beach with crystal clear turquoise water and a breath taking view. The bottom is soft sand providing easy access for swimming and snorkeling.

Facilities:

Picnic tables, changing area and garbage cans.

Comments:

The view from Honeymoon is similar to the view from Solomon. Add the top of Hans Lollik, the top of Congo Cay and Carval Rock to the list of visible islands.

There is good snorkeling along the rocks at either end of the beach.

Honeymoon may be more crowded than Solomon because it is a favorite destination of day charter boats.

Honeymoon is the beach featured on the front cover of this book.

CANEEL BAY

How To Get There:

Starting from Mongoose Junction go east 1.2 miles on Route 20. Turn left on the road leading into Caneel Bay Resort. Park in the parking lot to the left of the security booth and then check in at the Day Visitor Registration Booth.

Description:

Caneel Bay is a soft white sand beach typical of the north shore. There are coconut palms and sea grapes along the shoreline. The bottom is soft white sand.

Facilities:

Day guests at Caneel Bay Resort are asked to confine their visit to the Sugar Mill Restaurant, Beach Terrace Dining Room, Caneel Bay Bar, Caneel Bay Gift Shop, Watersports Shop, front desk/lobby area, Caneel Beach and Honeymoon Beach.

The beach chairs and lounges, towels, floats, sailboards, kayaks and sunfish sailboats are reserved exclusively for registered resort guests.

There is a bathroom available to day guests.

If you are visiting by boat you may tie up your dinghy at the dock on the west end of the beach. You must use a stern anchor.

Comments:

Caneel Bay first became a resort in the 1930's, and was the property of the West Indian Company Ltd. Lawrence S. Rockefeller purchased it in 1952. He developed the resort and then donated it to the Jackson Hole Preserve Corporation. This non profit organization also bought 5000 acres of surrounding land and donated it to the Federal Government to be used as a National Park.

Guests at Caneel Bay Resort can also use Scott Beach, Turtle Bay and Caneel Hawksnest.

You can frequently see turtles at Scott Beach, and the snorkeling between Scott Beach and Turtle Bay is excellent. Be careful; there can be a very strong current as well as boat traffic in this area.

HAWKSNEST

How To Get There:

Starting from Mongoose Junction go 1.8 miles east on route 20. Park in the Hawksnest parking lot.

Description:

Hawksnest is a beautiful north shore soft white sand beach. Behind the sand is a wall of seagrapes and coconut palms. The seagrapes bear fruit in the summer and can be quite tasty. The bottom is sandy with the exception of two areas of reef.

Facilities:

Hawksnest has a nice size parking area, although on some weekend afternoons, especially during season, it maybe difficult to find a place to park.

Between the parking area and the beach is a lovely wooded and shady area. There are two pavilions (covered decks with tables) that are often used for family parties, get togethers and meetings. These are available on a first come first serve basis after obtaining permission from the National Park. Uncovered picnic tables and barbecue grills are scattered throughout the area.

There are clean, but somewhat primitive toilet facilities, as well as a changing area. There is no running water, so no showers, sinks or flush toilets.

Comments:

Hawksnest seems to be the beach that attracts the most locals. The consensus of opinion is that this is due to the fact that Hawksnest is the first easily accessible, white sand beach that you come to upon leaving Cruz Bay. It also has the shortest walk from the parking lot to the beach, which is convenient for families with small children. Finally, Hawksnest is sheltered from the sometimes forceful tradewinds.

Hawksnest is another good beach for novice snorkelers because of the soft sandy bottom and the proximity of the reef. However, in the winter when the north swell is running, breaking surf may make swimming and snorkeling less inviting. On such days try Francis or Maho Bays which are free from ground sea.

Since Hawksnest faces east, it enjoys good morning sun. In late afternoon, especially in winter, the beach is in the shade and not as warm.

If you want to get away from the crowd and enjoy a more deserted beach, there is Little Hawksnest just a two minute rock scramble to the west, or left if facing the sea. Little Hawksnest is a sand beach with a sand and coral bottom.

Action Note:

Starting from the east end of Hawksnest, swim out around the red buoy to the white buoy, take a left, and swim to the seventh (last) white buoy. Turn around and swim back the way you came. Clock stops when you are out of the water, standing on the beach. The record for this event is 26:45.

OPPENHEIMER BEACH

How To Get There:

Oppenheimer Beach is 0.3 miles east of Hawksnest Bay or 2.1 miles east of Mongoose junction on Route 20. It will be the second driveway on your left after passing Hawksnest Beach. You can park by the chain across the driveway.

Description:

Oppenheimer Beach is a narrow beach at the extreme eastern end of Gibney Beach in Hawksnest Bay. There is some sand in front of the palm trees. The bottom is sand and reef.

Facilities:

Construction is under way for a community center.

Comments:

This beach is now known as Oppenheimer Beach after it's former owners the Oppenheimers. J. Robert Oppenheimer, the father of the atomic bomb, acquired the land from the Gibney's, the owners of the beach to the west. His widow, Kitty, gave the land to their daughter Toni.

Toni committed suicide and left it to the "people of St. John". This proved to be a nebulous entity, and as no provisions were made for the upkeep of the property, the house and land fell into disrepair. Graffiti covered the walls, and the house was vandalized by some of the less reputable citizens who occupied the premises.

This situation has recently been rectified, and construction is under way for a community center utilizing the old foundation of the Oppenheimer house. It will be dedicated in the summer 1994.

Oppenheimer Beach provides access to the best snorkeling on Hawksnest Bay along the rocks to the right.

From Oppenheimer Beach, which is rather narrow, the Gibney Beach can be accessed. Please respect the privacy of the Gibney family when using their beach. Do not trespass on their land which begins behind the line of first vegetation, and keep the area clean.

Dogs are not allowed, as with all beaches surrounded by swim buoys.

Gibney Beach was the location for the summer season segment of Alan Alda's movie, *The Four Seasons*, as well as various other movies and commercials.

HAWKSNEST EAST

How To Get There:

Park your vehicle in the parking lot at the Christ of the Caribbean which will be 0.5 miles east of Hawksnest Beach or 2.3 miles east of Mongoose Junction on Route 20 . Walk to the road and turn right. About fifteen yards on your right you will see a trail going down and off into the bush. Follow the trail until you see it fork at the side of a flamboyant tree.

The right fork involves ducking under a tree limb, climbing over a rock and avoiding a spiny bromeliad. There is a rope to help you up and down the last steep part of the trail. When you get to the bottom, the beach is to the left.

The left fork is somewhat more difficult. It takes you to a spot directly above the beach, but you will have to climb down the rocks to get there. It is an approximately fifteen foot nearly vertical decent to the beach below. There are, however, sufficient hand and foot holds to negotiate the climb.

These are not easy trails, and they can be dangerous. This route is not for everyone.

An alternative access to this beach is to snorkel or swim from Oppenheimer Beach.

Description:

Small cove with soft white sand and sand bottom.

Facilities: None

Comments:

This is probably St. John's smallest sand beach. When the surf is up or when the tide is particularly high, there is hardly any beach at all. On calm days and normal tides, though, this is a lovely little beach for picnics, swimming and snorkeling.

DENIS BAY

How To Get There:

According to Virgin Island law all beaches are available to the public. The public trust land extends from the water to the line of first vegetation. The land behind the vegetation at Denis Bay is privately owned and access to the beach from the road is prohibited by the owners. However, Denis Bay can be reached by boat. Be very careful to avoid areas of reef when entering the bay. Anchor in sand and swim ashore.

Description:

Denis Bay is a soft white sand beach with a soft sand bottom. There are areas of shallow reef on either side of the beach.

Facilities: None

Comments:

You must confine your visit to the to the line of first vegetation. Please respect the privacy of any people living in the houses in back of the beach, and please leave the beach in the condition you found it. The buildings date back to plantation days. On the east is the Great House. A little to the west of it is the old warehouse that has been converted into living quarters. On the western side of the beach are the remains of two slave cabins.

In the 1920's and 1930's there was a sport fishing club located at Denis Bay called the Deep Sea Fishing Club.

Denis Bay will become part of the National Park upon the death of it's present owner Julius Wadsworth.

Mr. Wadsworth commissioned St. Johnians Terrence Powell and Thomas Thomas to build the Christ of the Caribbean statue on Peace Hill in 1953.

JUMBIE BAY

How To Get There:

Heading east on the North Shore Road 2.5 miles from Mongoose Junction or 0.2 miles from the Christ of the Caribbean is the small parking area on the right side of the road for Jumbie Bay. Walk east to the wooden stairs on the left which descend to the trail leading to the beach.

Description:

Jumbie is a white sand beach. The bottom is a combination of sand, rock and reef.

Facilities:

Garbage cans are made available and emptied by the National Park Service.

Comments:

The word Jumbie, originally spelled Djambe, is an African word meaning supernatural being. They are similar to the Duppies of Jamaica and the Zombies of Haiti.

Jumbie Bay is a relatively small and uncrowded beach that offers good snorkeling and beautiful views. Looking out to sea you can see Jost Van Dyke, Green Cay, Whistling Cay, Trunk Cay and Great Thatch.

TRUNK BAY

How To Get There:

Trunk Bay is 3.0 miles from Mongoose Junction heading east on Route 20.

Park in the parking lot and walk past the taxi stand towards the beach.

You may see the taxi men playing an animated game of dominos while waiting for their clients.

Description:

Trunk Bay is the most visited and most developed of the St. John beaches. It can also be argued that it is the most beautiful.

Trunk Bay comes close to exemplifying perfection in the perception of what a beach should look like. It has a palm tree and sea grape fringed shoreline, a white powdery sand beach with a soft sandy bottom, crystal clear turquoise waters, cool breezes and fantastic views.

Facilities:

There is an underwater snorkeling trail in the vicinity of the island, Trunk Cay, not far from the beach. The Park has placed signs along the trail providing general information and identifying some of the flora and fauna common to the coral reef.

There is a shop which provides just about everything you might need while at the beach, such as snorkel equipment rental, sun screen, towels, insect repellent, hats, T shirts, bathing suits, film, batteries, books, post cards and souvenirs.

Other facilities include a snack bar, showers, bathrooms, changing areas, telephones, picnic tables and lifeguards. The pavilion is available for functions upon obtaining a permit from the National Park.

Comments:

In 1929 Erva and Paul Boulon Sr. bought Trunk Bay and 100 additional acres of land for $2500. The National Park acquired it from the Boulons in 1959.

If you don't need life guards, snack bars, shops and taxis, and you want to enjoy Trunk Bay in it's uncrowded and pristine state, all you have to do is arrive early in the morning (before 8:00 or 9:00) or late in the afternoon (after 4:00 or 5:00).

Since Trunk Bay faces west, it can be particularly beautiful late in the day.

Trunk Bay is sometimes subject to the breaking surf of the north swell in winter, making swimming and snorkeling less comfortable. Try Francis Bay as an alternative on these days. .

The brown animals that look like stretched out squirrels that you often see in Trunk Bay are mongooses. It is also very likely that you will encounter wild donkeys milling about.

Action Note:

The long stretch of sandy shoreline provides good jogging and long distance swimming when not crowded.

You can begin your day with the "Official Trunk Bay Morning Workout:"

(1) Jog the length of the beach and back.

(2) Swim the length of the beach and back.

(3) Do push ups in the sand by the water.

(4) Do sit ups or crunches in the sand by the water.

PETER BAY

How To Get There:

The entrance to Peter Bay Estate is at the top of the steep hill going east past Trunk Bay. The estate road and access to the beach are available only to homeowners and their guests. All others can reach the beach only by water.

Description:

Peter Bay is a somewhat narrow stretch of soft white sand beach with a soft sand bottom. There is a beautiful view and a cool breeze.

Facilities: None

Comments:

If you choose to visit Peter Bay, remember that the Public Trust lands extend from the water to the line of first vegetation. Please respect the privacy of the owners of the property behind the beach, and please leave the beach as you found it.

In the 1940's there was a shark liver oil factory at Peter Bay. Oldtimers say that on some summer days you could smell the aroma of shark liver oil as far away as Caneel Bay.

CINNAMON BAY

How To Get There:

Cinnamon Bay is 3.9 miles east of Mongoose Junction on Route 20. Park in the parking lot and walk to the beach.

Description:

Cinnamon Bay is typical of the north shore beaches with coconut palms, white soft sand and clear clean water with varying shades of blue. The bottom is soft and sandy. It is the longest continuous sand beach on St. John

Facilities:

Cinnamon has ample parking and regular taxi bus service to Cruz Bay. There is a restaurant, a snack bar and a general store. The Activities Desk offers snorkel trips, SCUBA lessons, day sails and cocktail cruises. There are rest rooms, changing rooms, showers, picnic facilities and telephones.

Cinnamon Bay has lifeguards on duty.

The Cinnamon Bay campground offers cottages, tents and bare camping sites.

At the end of the road to the beach you will find the Beach Shop, the Gift Shop and the museum. The Beach Shop rents snorkeling equipment, beach chairs, bikes, sea and surfing kayaks, windsurfers and sailboats. Just east of the Gift Shop is a beautiful kapok tree.

A self guided trail through some ruins and a beautiful trail that climbs through an aromatic bay rum stand to Centerline Road are located across the road from the main parking lot.

Comments:

Cinnamon Bay is probably the beach that has the most things to do. Not only is it the longest continuous sand beach on the island, but it is also the widest and the best for playing ball or frisbee on the beach. On Sundays locals organize pick up volleyball games beginning at about 11:00 in the morning.

There is good snorkeling around the island, Cinnamon Cay, just offshore.

Cinnamon is the only beach in St. John where surfers and experienced boogie boarders can take advantage of the north swell that comes in the winter.

Action note:

Rent a kayak from Rich Metcalf at the Beach Shop. Start seated in the kayak with one foot touching the sand. Paddle around the rocks at the west end of Cinnamon Cay and back to the beach. The clock stops when the bow of the kayak touches land. Be careful of reef and current when going through the narrow passage between Cinnamon Cay and the rocks. World record for this event is 4 minutes and 58 seconds.

LITTLE CINNAMON

How To Get There:

Follow the directions to Cinnamon Bay and walk down to the beach. Go left (west) and walk along the shoreline to the end of the beach where you will pick up a trail going through the bush. Continue along the trail, which goes over some rocks, until you reach the beach at Little Cinnamon.

Description:

Little Cinnamon is a soft white sand beach with a soft white sand bottom. Along the shoreline you will see maho trees, seagrapes, coconut palms, century plants, and philodendrons growing up the trunks of tall trees. On the eastern end of the beach there is a ruin of an old stone structure.

Facilities: None

Comments:

Little Cinnamon is a beautiful north shore beach with the added bonus of usually being secluded.

The view from the beach is superb and there is normally a nice breeze.

A trail from the center of the beach leads to the National Park VIP house, which is off limits to the public.

MAHO BAY

How To Get There:

Maho Bay is located about 1.25 miles past Cinnamon Bay or 5.2 miles past Mongoose Junction going east on Route 20. Park on the side of the road near the beach.

Description:

Maho Bay is a long and narrow white sand beach. The bottom is a combination of sand and grass.

Facilities:

There is a National Park pavilion on the extreme western portion of the beach. A permit must be obtained from the park in order to use this facility. This permit will also entitle you to use the bathrooms to the west of the pavilion which are otherwise locked and not available to the general public. The park will explain the rules and conditions pertaining to the use of the pavilion.

Comments:

The informality of this beach is what makes it special. It's right there by the side of the road, no parking lots or facilities, just a beach. Pull over and there you are.

In the summer the genip tree by the side of the road produces some of the sweetest genips in St. John.

At the eastern part of the beach there is a trail, called the goat trail, that leads to the Maho Bay Campground at Little Maho Bay.

Interestingly, Maho Bay, now a relatively narrow beach, was once one of the widest beaches in St. John. John Gibney and Ralph Powell, as well as other "horse kids", took advantage of this characteristic, as well as the great length of the beach, to have horse races on the sand.

FRANCIS BAY

How To Get There:

Continuing from Maho Bay about 1.5 miles from where the road leaves the beach and curves to the right, you will come to an intersection; turn left along the water's edge. Proceed to the stone building on the right at the intersection of the Francis Bay and Little Maho Bay Campground roads. You can park here and take the walking trail or continue straight to the end of the road and park by the beach.

If you are coming from Centerline road turn north at the Colombo Yogurt stand and right at the first intersection. This will take you to the intersection by the water where you will turn left and go to either the walking trail or the parking area by the beach.

The walking trail leads first to the northern end of the beach and is quite interesting. Along the way you will see the ruins of the historic Francis Bay Estate House and, somewhat further down the trail, an overlook with a view of the salt pond. This is an excellent place to bird watch. Along the trail there are genip trees which bear fruit in the summer. Near the beach are some big tamarind trees. Here you can go on to the beach or turn left to follow the trail along the edge of the salt pond. There are benches and a boardwalk along the shore of the salt pond where you can sit quietly and observe the life around this unique habitat. The trail continues to the road by the main parking area.

Description:

Francis Bay is a beautiful soft white sand beach with a soft sand bottom. The shoreline is fringed with sea grapes.

Facilities:

Facilities include toilets, located at the main parking area, picnic tables and barbecues.

Comments:

Francis Bay was formerly owned by the Francis family in the early 1900's. They operated a large cattle ranch there. Boats would come from as far away as Barbados and the Dominican Republic to buy their cattle.

Francis Bay is protected from the north swell and offers a quiet alternative to the other north shore beaches when the surf is up. It is also a good beach to go to on a windy day since it is sheltered from the prevailing tradewinds.

There is good snorkeling along the rocks at the northern shore. Avoid the deep water passage off Mary Point because of boat traffic and currents.

If you are going to the beach at Francis Bay, Little Maho or Waterlemon Bay, a visit to the restored Annaberg Sugar Mill will be well worth your while.

Action Note:

The road between Francis Bay and Waterlemon Bay is one of the few long stretches of relatively flat surface in St. John. This, combined with the spectacular views along the roadway, make it an excellent choice for runners and joggers who prefer not to run hills. After your run, you can take a swim along the shore of Francis Bay. It's an excellent way to start the day!

LITTLE MAHO BAY
(Maho Bay Campground)

How To Get There:

Continuing on from Maho Bay about 1.5 miles from where the road leaves the beach and curves to the right, you will come to an intersection; turn left along the waters edge. Proceed to the stone building on the right at the intersection of the Francis Bay and Little Maho Bay Campground roads. Turn left and go up the hill to the parking area. Day visitors are asked to check in at the registration desk located below the store.

Description:

The beach at Little Maho Bay is soft white sand and provides good swimming and easy snorkeling.

Facilities:

The campground has a restaurant, a general store, telephones and rest rooms. Windsurfers, kayaks, sunfish and snorkeling equipment can be rented at the activities desk where you can also arrange for lessons in the above activities.

Comments:

Before the Maho Bay Campground was built, Erva Boulon, the former owner of Trunk Bay and author of *My Island Kitchen*, built and ran a guest house at Little Maho Bay which was then called Lille Maho. Andy Rutnik, owner of Guavaberry Farms Nursery, and his wife, Janet Cook Rutnik, now an internationally recognized artist, used to be the caretakers of Lille Maho.

Ethel McCully, the author of *Grandma Raised the Roof*, also used to live in another part of Lille or Little Maho.

From the north end of the beach it is a short swim or rock scramble to a small quiet sandy beach between Francis Bay and the Little Maho Campground Beach.

Action Note:

On Sunday afternoons pick up volleyball is played from about 3:00 to 5:00.

WATERLEMON BAY
(Eastern Section Of Leinster Bay)

How To Get There:

To reach Waterlemon Bay follow the directions to Francis and Little Maho Bay, but turn right instead of left at the intersection by the waters edge. Continue along the shore to the parking lot on the right side of the road. After the lot the paved road turns right and up the hill to the Annaberg Sugar Mill, and the road along the shoreline turns to dirt. Here, either park in the lot and walk, or drive down the dirt track which continues along the shore. It is rugged and narrow. If you meet a vehicle going in the opposite direction, there may not be enough room to pass. A four wheel drive vehicle is recommended. Park at the end of the road by the beach.

Description:

There is a rock and sand beach with a rock and sand bottom at the end of the dirt road. There are also two small sand beaches with sand, reef and rock bottoms along the dirt track that leads to the larger rocky beach at the end of the dirt road.

Facilities:

You will find pit toilets and a trash bin near the parking lot.

Comments:

The best thing about the beach at Waterlemon Bay is it's proximity to the snorkeling around Waterlemon Cay, the island you see offshore. You can snorkel there from the beach, but it is a bit far. To decrease the snorkeling distance to the island, follow the trail at the far end of the beach. Bear left at the first fork in the trail which will continue to follow the shore line. At the end of the trail walk along the shore and choose a convenient place close to Waterlemon Cay and enter the water there. The snorkeling is excellent.

Waterlemon Bay is also the start of the Johnny Horn Trail

which goes to the Moravian Church at Coral Bay. There are spur trails to some very interesting ruins, and another unmaintained spur trail to Brown Bay. There is also a short trail that begins near the parking area that goes to the salt pond behind the beach.

CHAPTER TWO

South Shore Beaches

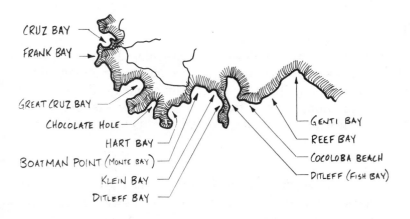

CRUZ BAY
FRANK BAY
GREAT CRUZ BAY
CHOLOLATE HOLE
HART BAY
BOATMAN POINT (MONTE BAY)
KLEIN BAY
DITLEFF BAY
GENTI BAY
REEF BAY
COCOLOBA BEACH
DITLEFF (FISH BAY)

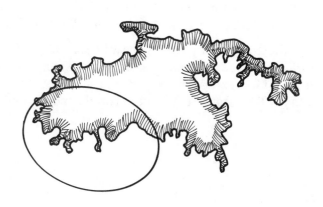

CRUZ BAY

How to get there:

Cruz Bay Beach is the beach along either side of the main ferry dock.

Description:

Cruz Bay is a white sand beach with a sand and grass bottom. The shoreline is fringed with coconut palms and seagrapes.

Facilities:

Cruz Bay is the main town in St. John. There are dumpsters and garbage cans, public bath rooms, and a dinghy dock for visiting sailors. In town are the government offices, police and fire stations, post office, National Park Visitor Center, library, museum, businesses, stores and restaurants.

Comments:

Cruz Bay Beach is a nice place to sit and enjoy the scenery and the activity of the harbor. It is not, however, good for swimming or water sports because of heavy commercial and pleasure boat traffic.

Cruz Bay was named after the Cross of the Crucifixion from the Spanish word Cruz which means Cross in English.

The illustration on page 35 shows Cruz Bay as it appeared in 1970. The wooden sailing vessel, Baby Mac, shown tied up along the old Cruz Bay dock, brought much of the cargo that came to St. John from St. Thomas, Tortola and beyond.

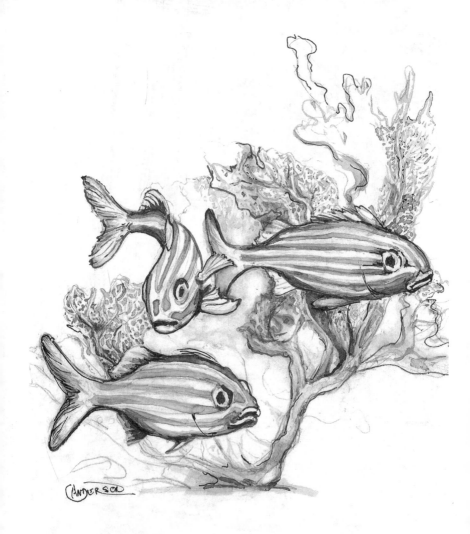

FRANK BAY

How To Get There:

Starting from the one way street that goes past Wharfside Village in Cruz Bay, turn right at the end of the road by the Catholic Church. Go about one quarter mile, bearing right until you get to the beach.

Description:

Frank Bay is a sand and rock beach. The bottom is coral and sand near shore and becomes sandy further out. Beware of sea urchins in the area of the coral reef.

Facilities: None

Comments:

Frank Bay is the closest swimming beach to Cruz Bay and is within easy walking distance. You will rarely find more than one or two people here.

Enjoy.the spectacular view from the beach while sitting in the shade of the mangrove tree. You can see the islands of Little St. James, Great St. James, St. Thomas, Stevens Cay, Thatch Cay, Hans Lolick, Grass Cay and Mingo Cay.

Be careful as it can be rough at times when the north swell is up, or when the wake of a ferry or other large vessel comes ashore.

Frank Bay is frequented almost daily by local legend and internationally famous opera star Ivan Jadan. Ivan enjoys playing with an octopus that lives in a hole in the reef.

GREAT CRUZ BAY
(Hyatt Hotel Beach)

How To Get There:

Starting at the Texaco Station in Cruz Bay go east 0.9 miles on Route 104. Turn right at the entrance to the Hyatt Hotel. Park in the hotel parking lot and walk to the beach.

Description:

Great Cruz Bay was originally a relatively shallow bay surrounded by mangrove wet lands with a mud bottom. The bay was dredged and sand was brought in to create the sandy beach that is now there. The depth increases gradually, and there are no sea urchins or reef to worry about. The water is not as clear as in some of the other bays. The bay is generally calm and free from the ground sea or breaking surf that is common on north shore beaches in the winter. The Hyatt has done an excellent job of landscaping, and the beach and grounds of the hotel are beautiful.

Facilities:

Day visitors can use the beach, but the facilities such as lounge chairs and beach equipment are for use by Hyatt guests only.

Facilities available to day visitors are the restaurants and the Splash Bar by the pool. Cash is not accepted at the Splash Bar. If you are not a guest at the hotel, you must use an American Express credit card or get a cash voucher at the front desk.

CHOCOLATE HOLE

How To Get There:

From the Texaco Station go 1.1 miles east on route 104. Turn right on Chocolate Hole East Road. Drive to the end of the black top road and park by the beach.

Description:

Chocolate Hole is a sand beach with a mud and grass bottom. The depth increases gradually.

Facilities: None

Comments:

The beach is mostly used by people from the neighborhood or by boaters who have their boats moored here.

Chocolate Hole offers access to excellent snorkeling along the rocks and reef of the southeastern shore.

HART BAY

How To Get There:

Take Route 104 east from the Texaco Station in Cruz Bay 1.1 miles. Turn right on Chocolate Hole East Road. Drive 0.25 miles and turn left on to Bovocoap Point Road, which is the last turn before the beach at Chocolate Hole. Drive about 0.3 miles to the intersection of Bovocoap Point Road and Hart Bay Overlook. Park on the side of the road at the Hart Bay Overlook. The trail goes behind the house named Poinciana. Walk 100 yards from the road to the beach.

Description:

Hart Bay is a sand and pebble beach with a rock, sand and reef bottom. It is most often frequented by residents of Chocolate Hole. The sea here can be rough as it is exposed to the easterly trades. The water is shallow and there are patches of reef and sea urchins, so be careful entering the water to swim or snorkel.

Facilities: None

Comments:

Hart Bay Beach is a relatively large beach and few people go there. Thus, it can offer seclusion and solitude. There is good snorkeling behind the reef when the seas are calm.

All beaches in the Virgin Islands are public from the water to the line of first vegetation. Access to the beaches from the land, however, may be controlled by the owners of the property adjacent to the beach. Presently the Chocolate Hole Owner's Association has not been restricting access to the beach at Hart Bay. If you are not an owner or guest of an owner of property in Estate Chocolate Hole, you will be using this access at your own risk; and the Chocolate Hole Owner,s Association may at anytime decide to restrict access to this beach.

BOATMAN POINT (MONTE BAY)

How To Get There:

Coming from the Texaco Station in Cruz Bay go east 1.5 miles on route 104. Turn right at the top of Century Hill to Boatman Point Road. Go 0.3 miles and then turn left on to Monte Bay Road. Continue 0.3 miles to the end of the road. Park and walk down the wooden stairs to the rocky beach below.

Description:

Monte Bay Beach is primarily rocky with some sand. It can be rough with waves breaking over patches of reef. The bottom is rocky with sea urchins, so be very careful if you go in the water.

Facilities: None

Comments:

The beach is seldom visited other than by residents of the Boatman Point development, and you will most likely be alone here. There is good shelling and beach combing along the rocky shoreline. There's a nice breeze and a place to sit along the wooden stairs.

The access to this beach is private property owned by the Boatman Point development. The owners have not presently been restricting access to the beach, but may at any time. Use this access at your own risk.

KLEIN BAY

How To Get There:

Starting from the Texaco Station take Route 104 east 1.6 miles. When the road forks, with the paved portion going up a steep hill to the left (Gifft Hill Road), and the right side becoming dirt (Fish Bay Road); bear right on the dirt road. Make the first right turn on to the concrete road which leads to Klein Bay. Make the second right turn and park at the end of the road. From there you will see two short paths, both leading to the beach.

Description:

The beach is made of small colorfully polished stones. The pebbles extend into the water along the shoreline for about twenty feet and up to a depth of about three feet. The bottom then changes to one of larger rocks and reef for about twenty feet before becoming the sand and grass bottom which characterizes the majority of the bay.

Facilities: None

Comments:

The name Klein Bay comes from the Dutch and German word *klein* meaning small.

There is excellent snorkeling along the rocks on both sides of the bay.

Klein Bay is seldom visited and usually offers seclusion and solitude.

Although the entrance into the water is a bit difficult, the swimming is good. Enter between the center and eastern portion of the beach. It is safe to walk on the pebble bottom. When that ends, swim or snorkel over the area of larger rocks to avoid the sea urchins.

Klein Bay is an alternative to north shore beaches during the winter when there is ground sea or breaking surf on the north side of the island.

The access to this beach is privately owned by the Estate Rendezvous Owner's Association, but it is not currently restricted. Use the beach access at your own risk.

Action Note:

Swim along the shoreline from Klein Bay to the sandy beach at Ditleff Bay. The world's record is 13:30.

DITLEFF BEACH

How To Get There:

Starting from the Texaco Station take Route 104 east 1.6 miles. When the road forks, with the paved portion going up a steep hill to the left (Gifft Hill Road), and the right side becoming dirt (Fish Bay Road); bear right on the dirt road. Go 0.6 miles to the concrete road on your right which goes to Klein Bay. Don't turn! You will notice a telephone pole to your right. Continue on Fish Bay Road which descends and curves towards the left. Turn right just before the next telephone pole. This will be a dirt road that extends about forty feet and ends with a mound of dirt. Leave your car here and continue on foot.

The trail follows an old road through a scrub forest. There are good examples of century plants (used for native Christmas trees when they bloom), other agaves and varieties of cacti.

A ten minute walk will bring you to a point where you will see trails off to the left and right. The narrow one to the right (west) leads to the northern end of Ditleff Beach. The trail to the left leads to a view of the eastern shore with a steep and somewhat dangerous path to the rocky beach below. If you continue straight on the main path you will come to another point with trails going to the left and right. The right path leads to the southern end of Ditleff beach. The left path leads to a rocky beach on the Fish Bay side of the point. The main path continues and over the next hill is a path to the left leading to another rocky beach on the Fish Bay Side.

Facilities: None

Description:

Ditleff Beach, on the western side, is a combination of sand and pebbles. The sea is gentle and the bottom is grass and sand.

The rocky beaches on the Fish Bay or eastern side are exposed to the trade winds and can have breaking surf.

Comments:

Hart, Monte, Klein and Ditleff Bays together make up the large bay called Rendezvous Bay. This bay got its name by being the rendezvous point used by pirates preparing to raid ships going in and out of Charlotte Amalie on St. Thomas.

The western beach offers good snorkeling between Ditleff and Klein Bays. Watch for turtles, remoras, squid and eagle rays.

You will rarely find many people here.

The beaches on the east offer good shelling and beach-combing but are not suitable for swimming.

The contrast between the rugged and windy eastern side of the point and the calm and serene western side is interesting and dramatic.

The access to Ditleff point is private, but at the present time the owners are not restricting access. There is (hopeful) talk about the entire peninsula being turned over to the Nature Conservancy or some similar agency which will preserve the pristine nature of the area.

COCOLOBA BEACH

How To Get There:

From the Texaco Station in Cruz Bay take route 104 east to Fish Bay Road. Continue to the end of the road, about 2.1 miles, always keeping the sea on your right. You will pass Guavaberry Farms Nursery. The road gets a bit steep and rugged toward the end, and four wheel drive and off road driving experience is highly recommended. Park at the Fish Bay dock at the end of the road.

From here continue on foot, again keeping the water on your right. It will be about a fifteen to twenty minute walk. Go into the mangroves, and you will pick up a trail which will lead to some rocks by the waters edge. Walk along the shoreline now characterized by a small shallow lagoon with waves breaking over the surrounding reef. At the end of the lagoon continue over the rocks until you see Cocoloba Cay and the beach.

Description:

The beach is sandy but not good for swimming. The water is shallow with many sea urchins among the rocks. There is generally a strong current and breaking surf.

Facilities: None

Comments:

This remote and rarely visited beach may be somewhat of an adventure to get to, but on the way you will have the opportunity to experience many diverse and unique aspects of St. John not ordinarily seen by most people.

Between the Fish Bay dock and Cocoloba Cay is a reef break that is suitable for surfing and boogie boarding when the surf is up. Be careful as the reef is extremely shallow.

On calm days experienced snorkelers will enjoy the diving around Cocoloba Cay. Caution is recommended. This beach is probably the most private of all St. John beaches. It offers excellent picnicking, shelling and beachcombing. Here you can enjoy solitude and reflect upon the dramatic beauty and power of the sea meeting the land.

REEF BAY BEACH

How To Get There:

Do not confuse this beach with the beach at the end of the Reef Bay Trail which is called Genti Bay.

From the Texaco Station in Cruz Bay take route 104 east to the Fish Bay Road. Go 1.7 miles to the intersection of Marina Drive and Reef Bay Road. Bear left on to Reef Bay Road and go up the hill. Turn left after the concrete strip, about 0.2 miles from the intersection. There will be a house on the corner with a large century plant growing next to a turpentine tree. Go 0.2 miles further and park on the right side of the road across from the house with the wood shingle roof and sides.

The path to the beach starts at the utility pole. The first part is steep. You will find a knotted rope there which you may find helpful. Be careful on the rest of the path as it can be tricky and slippery at times.

Description:

The beach is white soft sand. The bottom is sand, rock and coral reef. There is breaking surf and current so use caution if swimming or snorkeling here.

Reef Bay is a large bay on the south side of St. John between The White Cliffs on the east and Cocoloba Cay on the west. Only the western most portion can be accessed (almost) by road. A reef extends from one side to the other with only two exposed areas. One is the beach at the western end of the bay called Reef Bay. The other is in the center of the bay by the ruins of the Reef Bay Sugar Mill. It is called Genti Bay. A shallow lagoon lies between the reef and the sandy shore.

Facilities: None

Comments:

This western portion of Reef Bay does not have the reef protecting it. The breaking surf from the southeasterly swells provides good surfing and boogie boarding when the wind is out of the south. Be careful of patches of reef which sometimes are quite near the surface. Ask the locals about specific surfing information.

The beach is uncrowded and there is good snorkeling on the rare days when the water is calm.

Reef Bay beach is a turtle nesting area.

The Reef Bay Sugar Mill, Genti Bay, and the Reef Bay Trail can be accessed from Reef Bay Beach by walking along the shore in an easterly direction and later picking up the spur trail to the main Reef Bay Trail. See the section on Genti Bay for more specific directions.

GENTI BAY
(Reef Bay Sugar Mill)

How To Get There:

Getting to Genti Bay is half the fun. There are three land routes, all involving moderately strenuous hikes.

The most common way of getting to Genti Bay is by going down the Reef Bay Trail which begins 4.9 miles east of Cruz Bay on Centerline Road, or Route 10. It is 2.2 miles to the sugar mill and the beach at Genti Bay. You will pass through shady, moist forest and dry forest. You will see many examples of beautiful and interesting trees and plant life. The trail, which is maintained by the National Park, has signs detailing interesting aspects of the hike. You will pass alongside the ruins of four sugar estates and some abandoned farming communities. Along the way you may be able to find ripe genips and limes. There is a spur trail to the petroglyphs, which are mysterious rock carvings at the base of a waterfall. There is also a spur trail that leads to Lameshur Bay. This spur trail has yet another spur trail that goes to the Reef Bay Great House which is being restored by the National Park. At the end of the main trail are the restored ruins of the Reef Bay Sugar Mill and the beach at Genti Bay. The National Park Service provides guided hikes on a scheduled basis. For more information check at the National Park visitor center.

From Lameshur Bay the trail starts at the western end of the beach and meets the Reef Bay Trail after 1.8 miles. Turn left at the intersection of the two trails and go another 0.8 miles to the beach.

Genti Bay can also be reached from the western beach at Reef Bay by walking east along the sandy beach until you get to the red and white rocks at the point. From here it is a short and moderately easy scramble over the rocks rounding the point. You then walk along the shore, possibly ducking into the mangroves every now and then, to avoid walking in the water. On one of these short forays inland you may see some interesting ruins. Shortly after these ruins, and before you reach the rocks jutting into the sea, you can pick up a trail, often not well maintained, that leads to the bottom of the Reef Bay Trail in the area of the sugar mill and the beach.

Description:

Genti is a sandy beach with a grass and sand bottom.

Facilities:

Small picnic site and pit toilets.

Comments:

Be sure and visit the petroglyphs, the Reef Bay Sugar Mill and the Great House.

Bring insect repellent as there tends to be sand flies in the vicinity of the beach.

CHAPTER THREE

Beaches of Coral Bay South

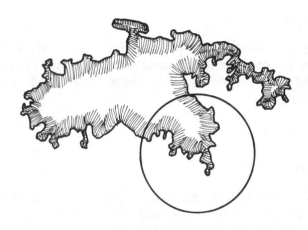

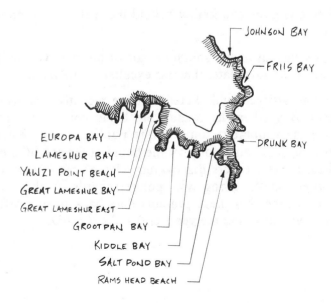

JOHNSON BAY

FRIIS BAY

EUROPA BAY

LAMESHUR BAY

YAWZI POINT BEACH

GREAT LAMESHUR BAY

GREAT LAMESHUR EAST

GROOTPAN BAY

KIDDLE BAY

SALT POND BAY

RAMS HEAD BEACH

DRUNK BAY

JOHNSON BAY

How To Get There:

Johnson Bay is 1.7 miles south of the Moravian Church on Route 107. Turn left on to the dirt road and park.

Description:

Along the coastline of Johnson Bay lies a coarse sand beach. The bottom is sand and coral. A narrow band of coral is located about ten feet out from the shore. This must be passed over carefully.

Facilities: None

Comments:

Johnson Bay is used mainly by people who have their boats moored out behind the reef, or who use this bay to launch windsurfers and other small craft.

There is good snorkeling behind the reef in calm protected waters.

Walking out to the southern part of the bay, you will find an area of shallow water that has excellent bone fishing.

Indian artifacts and skeletons were recently discovered at Johnson Bay when the roads were being constructed for the housing development south of the public access. When the excavation was being done for the house at the southern end of the beach, the workers discovered piles of old broken conch and whelk shells, along with pottery shards. Archaeologists have theorized that these remains date back to two different Indian civilizations in the years 600 and 1200 AD.

FRIIS BAY

How To Get There:

Take route 107 south 2.5 miles from the Moravian Church, and turn left when you see the sign for Lucy's Bar and Restaurant.

Description:

Friis Bay is a sand and rock beach. The bottom is a mixture of sand, rock and coral.

Facilities:

Lucy's Bar and Restaurant

Comments:

Lucy's Bar and Restaurant is a quaint and picturesque place to stop. Lunch is served between 11:30 and 5:00 and dinner between 5:30 and 8:30. Their specialty is delicious native style cuisine. Your meal will be prepared and served by Chef Alfred and his family. The atmosphere is friendly and relaxed.

You can eat inside or out by the beach in the shade of a beautiful sea grape tree. In addition to tables set out for lunch there is a bench and lounge chairs for use by the customers. There is also a game of horseshoes for those who want to play.

Lucy's restaurant is the only restaurant in St. John that compares in cuisine and ambiance to the West Indian style beachfront restaurants found in the British Virgin Islands.

The snorkeling is good around the patches of reef. Beware of sea urchins when entering the water.

The view down the island chain is spectacular, and the breeze is cool and refreshing. What's not to like?

SALT POND BAY

How To Get There:

To reach Salt Pond Bay take route 107 south 3.9 miles from the Moravian Church in Coral Bay. The 0.2 mile long trail to the beach begins at the parking area.

Description:

Salt Pond Bay is a soft white sand beach. The bottom is sand with areas of pebbles and grass.

Facilities:

Chemical toilet, picnic tables and barbecues.

Comments:

The National Park recommends extra water and a hat due to the particularly hot and sunny condition of the area.

There have been cases of thievery reported at Salt Pond Bay. Don't leave valuables unattended in your vehicle or at the beach!

In the winter when the ground sea is up, and the surf is breaking on the north shore beaches, Salt Pond Bay can be an alternative for those desiring a calmer white sand beach with easy access.

Two interesting trails begin at the south end of the beach.

The Drunk Bay Trail is 0.3 miles long and goes by the salt pond. Salt can be harvested there when the weather is dry, (usually around June and July).

This trail leads on to the rocky and windswept beach at Drunk Bay. The beachcombing is excellent, but beware of dangerous swimming conditions.

The Ram Head Trail is 0.9 miles long and passes by a blue cobblestone beach. The trail goes on to Ram Head Point two hundred feet above sea level with sheer rocky cliffs descending to the Caribbean. The views from the point are dramatic and spectacular.

Action Note:

Old legends say Ram Head is a special and magical wishing point. Throw a rock from the top of the cliff, and shout out a wish as loud as you can while your rock is in the air. If you finish shouting your wish before the rock hits the water, and if your rock hits the water without hitting the cliff or other rocks, your wish will come true. The rules for wishing as outlined by the genie in the movie "Aladdin" apply. (This means no wishing for more wishes, wishing for people to fall in love, etc.). Personal experience has shown that this legend is real, and a well thrown rock, coupled with a fast, loud, wish, will make a wish come true.

KIDDLE AND GROOTPAN BAYS

How To Get There:

Take route 107 south 4.2 miles from the Moravian Church in Coral Bay. Turn left on to the dirt road. Go 0.3 miles and turn right where the road forks. When the road forks again, a little past the first fork, turn left and go 0.1 miles to Kiddle Bay or turn right and go 0.2 miles to Grootpan Bay.

Description:

Kiddle and Grootpan are both cobblestone beaches. The cobblestone bottom extends relatively far out into the bay before changing to sand and grass.

Facilities: None

Comments:

The beaches of Kiddle and Grootpan Bays are rarely visited. They offer picnicking, beachcombing, snorkeling and a chance to get off the beaten track.

The salt pond behind the beach at Grootpan Bay is the largest on the island and salt can be harvested when weather conditions are right.

Herons like to fish along the exposed reef at Kiddle Bay.

GREAT LAMESHUR BAY

How To Get There:

At the end of route 107 south continue 0.6 miles on the dirt road. You can park near the big tamarind tree at the opening to the beach. This road becomes very steep and rutted. A four wheel drive vehicle and off road driving experience is necessary. As a matter of fact, most rental car agencies have declared this section of road "off limits".

For those who choose not to negotiate this rough section of road, park at the bottom of the hill and continue on foot.

Description:

Great Lameshur is a large cobblestone beach with a rocky bottom.

Facilities: None

Comments:

Great Lameshur is usually secluded. It provides access to good snorkeling and exploring.

A fifteen minute rock scramble along the eastern shore will take you to an isolated cobblestone and sand beach which provides privacy, picnicking, swimming and snorkeling. It's truly an idyllic spot and worth the extra effort it takes to get there.

LAMESHUR BAY

How To Get There:

At the end of route 107 south continue one mile on the dirt road. You can park anywhere along the road in the vicinity of the beach. This road becomes very steep and rutted. A four wheel drive vehicle and off road driving experience is necessary. As a matter of fact, most rental car agencies have declared this section of road "off limits".

For those who choose not to negotiate this rough section of road, park at the bottom of the hill and continue on foot.

Description:

Lameshur is a beautiful white sand beach with a sand, pebble and grass bottom.

Facilities:

There are picnic tables, barbecues and toilet facilities.

Comments:

On the western end of the beach are some ruins as well as the entrances to the Reef Bay and Bordeaux Mountain Trails. On the grassy area you may find a lone, bent over, scrawny sugar apple tree which, despite it's sad appearance, bears great fruit.

On the eastern end of the beach is the Yawzi Point Trail. People infected with the disease yaws, an infectious tropical disease causing destructive skin and bone lesions, were once forced to live here.

The 0.3 mile trail passes through thorny scrub vegetation. It ends at a rocky point where there is a spectacular view of the southern Caribbean shore of St. John. If you look carefully you may notice a spray of orchids growing on the eastern side of the trail.

About half way down the trail there is a short spur trail to the east which leads to a unique isolated cove which is well worth a visit.

Lameshur tends to be less crowded than the popular north shore National Park beaches due to it's difficult access and remoteness.

EUROPA BAY

How To Get There:

Europa Bay can be reached by hiking the Lameshur Bay Trail. This trail originates at the western end of Lameshur Bay and is marked with a National Park sign. About 0.5 miles up the trail there is a 0.3 mile spur trail, also marked by a sign, which leads to Europa Bay.

Description:

Most of the beach is cobblestone and coral, with the exception of a small sandy area at the extreme northern end. The bottom is rocky.

Facilities: None

Comments:

Europa Bay is uncrowded, pristine and dramatic.

The spur trail to the beach passes by a beautiful salt pond which can provide good bird watching.

The snorkeling is best on calm days when the water is not churned up. Be careful entering the water.

CHAPTER FOUR

East End Beaches

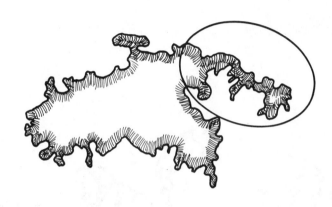

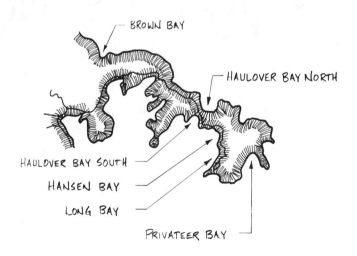

BROWN BAY

HAULOVER BAY NORTH

HAULOVER BAY SOUTH

HANSEN BAY

LONG BAY

PRIVATEER BAY

BROWN BAY

How To Get There:

Starting from the Coral Bay Moravian Church, go east 1.1 miles on Route 10. You will pass Estate Zootenvaal and then cross a small concrete bridge. Turn left just after the bridge and park on the dirt road. Twenty yards up the road you will come to a fork. As Yogi Berra, the famous baseball player, once said, "When you get to the fork in the road; take it!" The right fork is the beginning of the Brown Bay Trail. It is a 0.8 mile hike to the beach.

Brown Bay can also be reached by taking the Brown Bay spur trail off the Johnny Horn Trail. The Johnny Horn Trail connects Waterlemon Cay and the Moravian Church in Coral Bay. The Brown Bay spur trail is not maintained and can be very unfriendly because of the abundance of thorny "catch and keep" bushes.

Description:

The beach at Brown Bay is narrow and is composed of sand and pebbles. The bottom is reef, sand and grass.

Facilities: None

Comments:

An abundance of flotsam washing up along the beach, provides excellent beachcombing.

Brown Bay offers the opportunity to enjoy superb views and cool breezes in a natural and private setting.

The water tends to be shallow, but there is access to good snorkeling. Beware of sea urchins when entering the water.

HAULOVER

How To Get There:

Haulover is 3.0 miles past the Coral Bay Moravian Church going east on Route 10. Park by the side of the road. Here, on the south side, there is a sand and coral beach. To reach Haulover Bay on the north, take the trail on the north side of the road. The trail is over flat terrain and is about 150 yards long.

Description:

The beach by the side of the road on the south is sand and coral with a sand and rock bottom.

The beach at the end of the trail on the north side of the road has varying characteristics. The western portion is rocky with a rock bottom. On the eastern end of the beach, you will find two narrow sandy beaches with grassy bottoms. The shoreline is lined by seagrape and mangrove trees.

Facilities: None

Comments:

The beach is secluded and has a nice view and a cool breeze.

Haulover's name comes from it's unique topographical characteristics. A narrow and flat strip of land separates the bay on the Coral Bay side from the bay on the north side. It was, and still is, relatively easy to haul small boats over this stretch of land. The alternative would be to sail upwind for over two miles, and then round the point at East End. This area is notorious for strong currents and rough seas. In the days of pirates and buccaneers a small vessel being pursued by a larger vessel could "haul over" their boat to the other side, thus eluding the enemy vessel, which would have to spend hours sailing around East End.

The land behind the high water mark of the beach on the eastern side is privately owned.

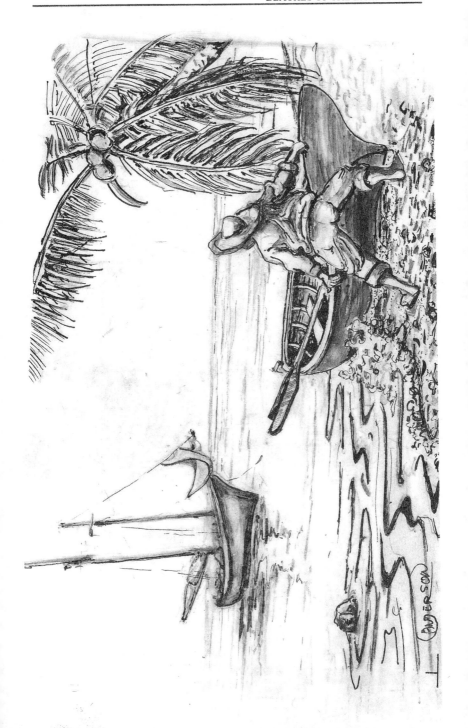

HANSEN BAY
(Vie's Snack Shop)

How to Get There:

Vie's Snack Shop is located 3.7 miles east of the Moravian Church on route 10.

Description:

The beaches at Hansen Bay are composed of sand and pebbles. The bottom of the bay is a mixture of sand rock and grass.

Facilities:

Vie's Snack Shop is open Tuesday through Saturday 10:00 AM - 5:00 PM.

Snacks include conch fritters, garlic chicken (Trinidad Charlie's favorite!), johnny cakes, island style beef patty and home made pineapple and coconut tarts. Sodas, beer and other cold drinks are also available.

Comments:

The beaches of Hansen Bay are privately owned. If you are visiting them by land you must first ask permission. Many times Vie will open the gate to the beach for use by the customers of the Snack Shop.

About a quarter mile east from Vie's Snack Shop is a small beach where access is not restricted by a gate. It is also owned by Vie's family. Vie asks that if there are people at home across the road, you ask their permission to use the beach. If no one is home, "Please go ahead and enjoy the beach."

The sailing vessel that you sometimes see anchored out in the bay belongs to local artist, celebrity and illustrator of this book, Les Anderson.

Christine Singer visited Vie's Snack shop, and she wrote this about the visit:

"Vie is a friendly and gracious lady. She made me feel welcome and comfortable.

When I first arrived, the Snack Shop was open but unattended except for a big black and white cat lazing on the table, and some chickens pecking around the way they do. In no time a woman's voice called to me saying that she would be right there. It was Vie. She had been walking across the street near the beach showing some visitors things of interest, such as local plants, flowers, a large tamarind tree, some goats and the chickens. They loved the chickens and the fat cat.

The scene reminded me of the friendliness and hospitality typical of the native St. John culture that captured my heart so many years ago.

I can understand why everyone on the East End knows and loves Vie."

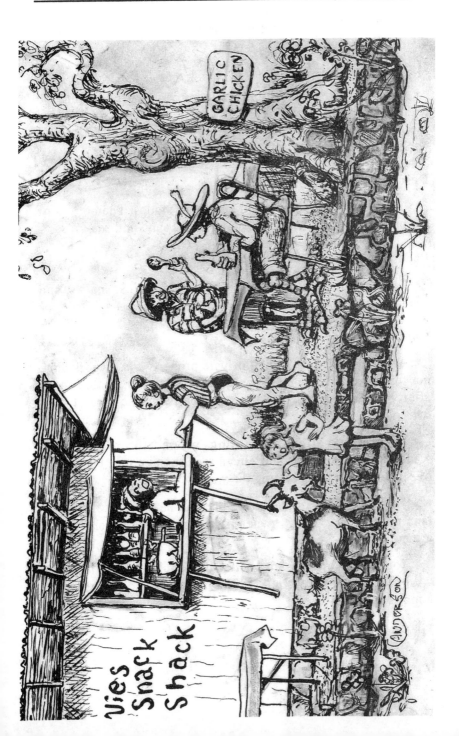

LONG BAY

How To Get There:

From the Coral Bay Moravian Church go east on Route 10 to the end of the road and park by the dumpster. Take the trail which goes to the beach and runs between the trailer and Newfound Cottage.

Description:

The beach consists of sand and small stones. The bottom of the bay is rocky at first and then becomes sand and sea grass.

Facilities:

The End of the Road Stand offers cold drinks, snacks, and friendly service.

Comments:

Although the beach is on private property the owners have not restricted access. You should act respectfully, and clean up after you leave. You will, of course, be using the area at your own risk.

There is excellent snorkeling, around the rocks at the southern shore and around Pelican rock to the north. Be careful of sea urchins when entering the water.

There is a dock on the beach that can be used for fishing or landing a dinghy, if the owners or guests of the beach cottage are not using it.

You will also find a number of beautiful old tamarind trees with particularly tasty fruit. (If you like the bitter sweet taste of tamarinds.)

PRIVATEER BAY

How To Get There:

Take route 10 east almost to the end of the road. As you are coming down the last hill, turn left at the sign that reads Privateer Bay Estates. Proceed up the dirt road 0.2 miles, and then turn left on the paved road. Follow this road to the end. A four wheel drive vehicle is essential in order to negotiate the last section of the road which is unpaved and rugged.

Description:

Privateer Bay is a remote and rocky beach with a rocky bottom.

Facilities: None

Comments:

Privateer Bay is a secluded and pristine rock beach. On the rare calm days there is excellent snorkeling along the rocks on the north end of the beach. Usually it is quite rough, especially when the wind is out of the south, making for poor and dangerous snorkeling conditions. Entry into the water is difficult and should be attempted only by experienced divers. Watch out for sea urchins!

Privateer Bay is owned by Privateer Bay Estates and is private property. Access is not being restricted at this time. Kindly respect the pristine nature of the area and leave it as you found it. Please do not remove any shells or coral!

Afterword

If you have any additional information or contributions concerning St. John beaches please write and let me know. Also please inform me if you have set any new world's records either from my action notes or from events of your own.

Additional copies of *The St. John Beach Guide* may be ordered by sending a check or money order for $9.95 per copy along with your name and address to:

Sombrero Publishing Company
PO Box 1031
St. John VI 00831

Appendix

Soft white sand beaches with soft sand bottom, easy entry:

Solomon, Honeymoon, Caneel, Hawksnest, Gibney,
Trunk, Cinnamon, Little Cinnamon, Maho,
Little Maho, Francis, Salt Pond, Lameshur

Beaches With Lifeguards:

Trunk Bay, Cinnamon Bay

Beaches with toilet facilities:

Caneel Bay, Hawksnest, Trunk Bay, Cinnamon Bay,
Francis Bay, Little Maho Bay, Great Cruz Bay, Genti
Bay, Friis Bay, Salt Pond Bay, Lameshur Bay

Beaches with showers:

Trunk Bay, Cinnamon Bay

Best snorkeling:

Waterlemon Bay, Chocolate Hole, Klein Bay, Scott to
Turtle Bay (Caneel Bay guests or by sea only)

Surfing or Boogie Boarding Beaches:

Reef Bay (South Swell), Between Cocoloba Cay and
the Fish Bay dock (South Swell), Cinnamon Bay
(North Swell)

Beaches With Action Notes:

Solomon Bay, Hawksnest Bay, Trunk Bay, Cinnamon
Bay, Francis Bay, Little Maho, Klein Bay, Salt Pond
Bay

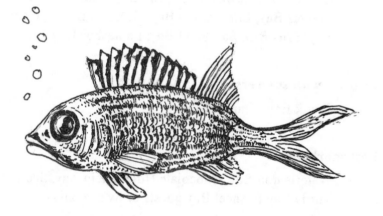

Index of Beaches